THE TU
GARDEN
1485–1603

Twigs Way

SHIRE PUBLICATIONS

Published in Great Britain in 2013 by Shire Publications Ltd, Midland House, West Way, Botley, Oxford OX2 0PH, United Kingdom.

43-01 21st Street, Suite 220B, Long Island City, NY 11101, USA.

E-mail: shire@shirebooks.co.uk   www.shirebooks.co.uk

© 2013 Twigs Way.

A CIP catalogue record for this book is available from the British Library.

Shire Library no. 720.   ISBN-13: 978 0 74781 214 2

Twigs Way has asserted her right under the Copyright, Designs and Patents Act, 1988, to be identified as the author of this book.

Designed by Tony Truscott Designs, Sussex, UK and typeset in Perpetua and Gill Sans.

Printed in China through Worldprint Ltd.

13 14 15 16 17   10 9 8 7 6 5 4 3 2 1

COVER IMAGE
The recreated Tudor Gardens at Kenilworth exemplify colour and pattern and Renaissance introductions. (Getty Images.)

TITLE PAGE IMAGE
Detail from Adam Lonicer's (1557) *Krauterbuch* of a plantsman's garden.

CONTENTS PAGE IMAGE
In collectors' gardens, flowers were planted as individuals, rather than in groups, so that each could be individually admired. Raised beds also brought the plants closer to their admirers, as in this flower garden portrayed in the 1594 edition of Thomas Hill's *The Gardener's Labyrinth*.

IMAGE ACKNOWLEDGEMENTS
Images are acknowledged as follows: The Warden and Fellows of All Souls College, Oxford (Codrington Library), page 28 (top); Buckinghamshire County Council, page 36; Cressing Temple Tudor Garden, pages 30, 32–3 and 40–1; The Devonshire Collection, page 34; English Heritage, pages 43, 46 (top right), 56–7; Essex Record Office/Essex County Council, page 9; Friends of Nonsuch Palace, page 61; the Garden Museum, title page, contents page and pages 4, 6 (top), 7 (all), 8 (top), 12, 15, 17, 18, 19, 20, 21, 22, 23, 24 (both), 25 (top), 27, 39, 46 (bottom) and 47; Mary Evans Picture Library, page 55; The National Trust, page 31; The National Trust/Bridgeman Art Library, pages 44, 48; Northamptonshire Record Office, page 8 (bottom); The owners of Otley Hall, pages 28 (bottom), 37 and 50; The Royal Collection/The Bridgeman Art Library, page 53; Royal Museums Greenwich/ Bridgeman Art Library, pages 49; Tudor Gardens and House, Southampton, pages 11, 29 and 54.

All other images are the author's own.

The images from Gerard's *Herball* on pages 17, 19, 20, 21, and 22 were hand coloured in the modern period.

Shire Publications is supporting the Woodland Trust, the UK's leading woodland conservation charity, by funding the dedication of trees.

CONTENTS

The firſte Booke,

teacheth the ſkilfull ordering and care, to be beſtowed on Gardens , with the neceſſary helpes, defences, and ſecretes, vvhich this at large vttereth.

VVhat thre pointes are to be lerned (of euery Gardener) minding to haue a fruitful Gardē, the health that may be recouered by vvalking in the ſame : and the commoditie of Gardés, placed neare to the Citie.

SEing a fruitful and pleaſaunt Garden, cā not be had, without the good ſkill, & diligente mynde of ẏ Gardiner (or maiſter of the grounde)

neither can any profite ariſe by Gardening without coſt and charges therein beſtowed: neither parfitly can it be attained vnto without Arte, inſtructinge the due ſeaſons of the yeare. It is therfore mete, that theſe thinges be firſt cared for, prouided and knowen , whiche being done, the Garden is made perſit, delectable, and profitable . And we then

C   receiue

What maner of maiſter or Gardiner a fruitful gardē requireth.

INTRODUCTION

There lavish Nature, in her best attire,
Powres forth sweet odors and alluring sightes;
And Arte, with her contending, doth aspire
T'excell the naturall with made delights:
And all, that faire and pleasant may be found,
In riotous excesse doth there abound.

Edmund Spenser (1591) *Muiopotmos (or the Fate of the Butterflie)*

FROM THE CORONATION of Henry VII in 1485 until the death of Elizabeth I in 1603, the Tudor period was one of revolutionary change. Renaissance, reformation, empire and exploration combined to transform the lives and gardens of all but the very poorest in society. New plants from the old and new worlds, and new concepts from the classical and renaissance worlds, created opportunities for change whether in the most basic of productive gardens, or the magnificent extravagance of courtier and royal gardens. Our sources for the history of gardens also increase in this period. Maps and surveys, 'views', books, letters and even archaeology provide us with insights into the design and planting of the Tudor garden, as well as first-hand accounts of the garden 'experience'. The scents and sounds, the sights, and the sheer excitement of the new are all captured in the words of travellers, courtiers, poets, and even gardeners, of the Tudor period.

It is with the words of gardeners, or at least garden writers, that the day-to-day workings of the 'typical' Tudor garden are known to us, as the sixteenth century saw the birth of the garden book, and a consequent flourishing of manuals giving instruction in all aspects of planning, planting and even the philosophy of gardens. The first 'popular' English gardening book appeared in 1563, written, or at least compiled, by Thomas Hill, an astrologer and book translator. Entitled *A most brief and pleasaunte Treatyse, teachynge how to Dresse, Sowe, and set a Garden*, the book was aimed primarily at the literate 'middling' classes, the owners of small manor houses with

Opposite:
The first page
of an early edition
of Thomas Hill's
*The Proffitable Arte
of Gardening*. This
work was based
on his popular
*Briefe and
Pleasaunte Treatyse*
on gardening,
which had been
printed in 1563.

Thomas Hill's popular works give us an insight into the day-to-day operations in the Tudor garden, as well as glimpses of tools and tasks we still recognise today. This woodcut reminds us that gardens were for play as well as work, with a small raised 'bowling green' in the background.

Using summer plants known in the sixteenth century, it is possible to create a jewel-box-like knot garden in the style favoured by the Tudors.

combined productive and decorative gardens. The book was so popular that, under the rather catchier title *The Profitable Arte of Gardening* (1568 onwards), it was reprinted in numerous editions. Hill's aim was to gather together in one book all the existing advice on gardening contained in the myriad classical works on plants and the more recent works on estate husbandry and farming, adding the usages of plants gained from books on herbs and physic. He added into this heady mix his own years of gardening experience, in the seasonal tasks to be carried out, and tools necessary for those tasks. The final work (by no means the 'Briefe' treatise of its title) provided a complete guide

for the Tudor gardener and garden owner, and also, through the woodcuts that accompanied later editions, a vision of the ideal Tudor garden. Building on his own popularity, although using the jocular pseudonym Didymus Mountain, Hill also brought out *The Gardener's Labyrinth* (1577), a title indicating labyrinthine knowledge, rather than designs for labyrinths, although it does include patterns for knot gardens. Hill dedicated *The Gardener's Labyrinth* to perhaps the most famous Tudor statesman and 'gardener', William Cecil (Lord Burghley) (1520–98), who thus forms a link between Hill and the other most famous writer of the period, John Gerard. Gerard (1545–1611), whose *Herball, or General Historie of Plantes* was written in 1597, was gardener to William Cecil at his house at Theobalds, where some of the rarest plants in the country could be found under his care.

Games such as bowls, archery or Troco (shown here) were an important element of the enjoyment of gardens in the Tudor period, shown here in a painting of the late sixteenth or early seventeenth century.

This rare Tudor watering pot fills by being immersed in water; by then placing a thumb over the top hole a vacuum is created so that the water can be carried. When the thumb is removed, the water streams out of the multiple holes in the base.

Despite the clearly recognisable tools and actions from this sixteenth-century gardening text, and the 'fashionable' raised beds, the planting style is very different from today. Individual plants were often accorded space to be admired at all angles. Here pride of place is being given to the Crown Imperial and other bulb plants.

This 1587 plan of the gardens at Holdenby House (Northamptonshire) by Ralph Treswell allows us an insight into the layout of a 'typical' Tudor garden. A long green forecourt and gatehouse lead to the house itself. The gardens around the house comprise orchards, bowling alley, and knot garden, all surrounded by wooden pale fence and set within a park.

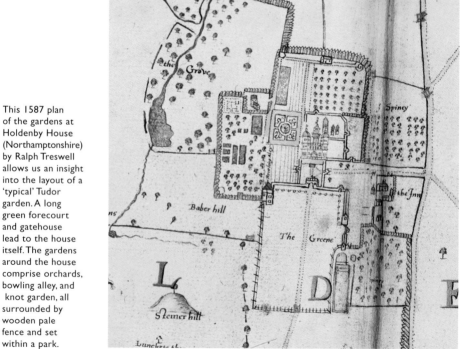

The Tudor gardening world was a small one, and also linked to William Cecil was Francis Bacon, the opening to whose *Essay on Gardens*, that 'God Almighty first planted a garden and indeed it is the purest of human pleasures' has been much quoted by gardeners ever since. Born in 1561, Bacon, son of Cecil's sister Anne, was as much an Elizabethan as a Jacobean and had been a confidante of the ill-fated Robert Devereux, Earl of Essex. Although his *Essay* was published in 1625, the gardens Bacon describes in it as being 'the greatest refreshment of the spirits of man' are full of Elizabethan plants and features. Cowslip, columbine, woodbine, and strawberries share beds (if not seasons) with the new arrivals including tulips, fritillaries, and the African Marigold. Allées lead through knot gardens (ill regarded by Bacon as 'but toys'), banqueting houses sit amongst fruit trees, and raised banks allow views over the jewel-like beds. Bacon and Cecil were also among the first to use the classical loggia, a feature that became popular in houses of the period to connect house and garden. Fountains and 'devices for arching water' also formed part of Bacon's fictional gardens, but statues were, as with most Tudor and Elizabethan gardens, a rarity, thought of only by princes and 'nothing to the true pleasure of a garden'.

Alongside the books and essays on rare plants, knot designs and princely gardens, came more practical books, concerned with the kitchen garden.

The gardens and orchards at Thorndon Hall (Essex) were created by Sir William Petre, Secretary of State for Henry VIII, Mary I, Edward VI and Elizabeth I. The gardens he created included some of the most fashionable Tudor features.

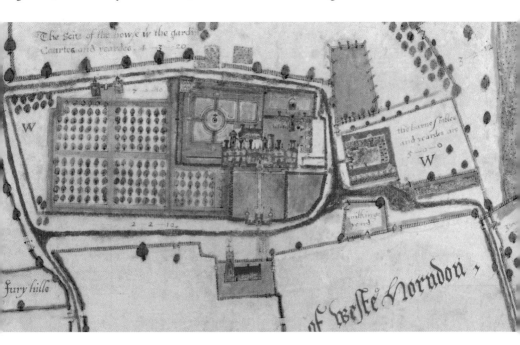

Richard Gardiner of Shrewsbury wrote of cabbages, parsnips, beans, onions and leeks in his *Profitable Instructions for the Manuring, Sowing and Planting of Kitchen Gardens*. Writing in 1599 when it was said that vegetables had gained greater popularity in England than ever before, Gardiner saved his greatest praise for the carrot, hailing them as an excellent saviour against wartime

siege and a blessing from God. Various other authors also translated works from the French and the Dutch, most notably Barnaby Goodge's *Four Bookes of Husbandry* (1577) and Richard Surfleet's *Countrie Farm* (1600), whilst Gervase Markham covered husbandry, housekeeping and horsemanship. Thomas Tusser gave instruction to both the countryman and his country housewife in his *Five Hundred Pointes of Good Husbandry* in 1573. Tusser envisages a world away from the banqueting houses and water spouts, sending his country housewife to collect herbs, flowers and strawberry plants from the wild and set them back in the garden. However, even the country housewife had the ubiquitous 'gilleflowers' (literally July flowers), and set them in amongst 'the knot and the border and rosemarie gaie'.

Tusser's Tudor garden was a hard-working one, where the women of the house were 'setting and sowing' from morning till night, providing medicines and foods for the household, and there is little evidence of pleasure gardens, or the new rarities, whether flower or vegetable. For many, however, the essence of the sixteenth-century garden will be forever captured not in these practical works, but in the world of poets and playwrights including Edmund Spenser (1552–99), John Donne (1572–1631) and, of course, William Shakespeare (1564–1616). Whether they were celebrating the everlasting spring of the reign of Elizabeth, or building visions of a fairy paradise, flowers were the stock of any writer in this period. Charged with meaning and double meanings understood by readers and listeners, Spenser's 'Coronations and Sops in Wine, Worn of Paramours' mixed with Ophelia's rosemary for remembrance, rue for regret, and the faithful violet. Again these were the traditional plants of Tudor England, plants that over the generations had taken on meaning and place in the seasonal round of life. Primroses for springtime dalliance, roses for summer love, cherries for virginity ripe to be picked. Elizabeth herself was portrayed with two cherries in her hair in the 'Pelican portrait' by Nicholas Hilliard, whilst Shakespeare writes of spring flowers that, like old maids, die before the sun in all his strength has touched them. Fantasy gardens filled prose and poetry, from Spenser's *The Faerie Queene* and Philip Sidney's *Arcadia*, to the garden scenes in Shakespeare's *Richard II* where England itself is compared to a sea-walled garden: 'Her fruit-trees all upturned, her hedges ruin'd, her knots disorder'd and her wholesome herbs swarming with caterpillars'. For better or for worse, gardens, plants and flowers played a central role in Tudor life, landscape and culture, from the humble housewife to the royal court.

Opposite: Waiting to burst forth in flower: this recreated Tudor garden demonstrates the importance of the summer months to gardens filled with traditional flowers. The introduced bulbs and rarities of the Elizabethan period will soon bring colour to spring and autumn plantings.

Bright flowers contrast with grey foliage in the knot gardens at the recreated Tudor House and Garden, Southampton.

PLANTING PARADISE

To Paradise right well comparable,
Set all about with floures fragrant

Stephen Hawes, *c.* 1506

DESPITE THE SUPPLEMENTATION of our native plants by first the Romans, then monastic influences, and finally Crusaders and traders, at the start of the Tudor period even the most lavish of gardens would have contained a selection of herbs, flowers and fruits that were almost exclusively European. Woodbine, holy-hocks, roses, sweet-rocket and mary-golds jostled with pinks, pansies and 'bouncing bet' (the traditional name for soapwort) in the most floral garden, whilst for the labourer the familiar staples of leeks and coleworts, lovage and rue, might only be cheered by flowers of native dog rose and wild violets. But as the Tudor world expanded, so did their gardens. Flowerbeds were transformed in the sixteenth century by introductions from Spain, Portugal, Turkey and eventually Mexico, Peru and the Americas. From the first snowdrops of spring to the *Nigella damascena* of high summer (brought from the Near East, as its name betrays), the garden was alive with exotics. 'Tulipmania' swept through the low countries and reverberated into England, alongside *Ranunculus*, *Laburnum* and *Lauristinus*, whilst the erotic 'love apple' vied with the Judas Tree and the passion flower in the gardens of the committed plant collector.

It was the 'discovery' and exploration of the New Worlds and their eventual colonisation that brought a colourful abundance of flowers, fruits and vegetables to England, along with a rush of apothecaries, botanists, and the first real plant collectors. Whether they came direct from the Americas or via the competing colonisers of Spain and Portugal, as fast as plants arrived they were seized upon by a plant-hungry nation. These were supplemented by the riches of Russia, Asia and the Orient brought in by companies such as the Muscovy Company (founded in 1550). Prior to the 1530s, the natural home of these new plants would have been the monasteries, with their wealth

Opposite:
The Crown Imperial, tulip and hyacinth were all regarded as collectors' flowers by the end of the sixteenth century, as shown here in Collaert's *Florilegium* of 1590.

13

The wholsome saulge, and lavender still gray, Ranke-smelling rue, and cummin good for eyes, The roses raigning in the pride of May, Sharpe isope, good for greene wounds remedies, Faire marigoldes, and bees-alluring thime, Sweete marioram, and daysies decking prime: Coole violets, and orpine growing still, Embathed balme, and chearfull galingale, Fresh costmarie, and breathfull camomill, Dull poppie, and drink-quickning setuale, Veyne-healing verven, and hed-purging dill, Sound savorie, and bazil hartie-hale, Fat colworts, and comforting perseline Colde lettuce, and refreshing rosmarine.

Edmund Spenser, *Muiopotmos*

(Saulge = sage; setuale = valerian; perselin = purslane.)

Edmund Spenser's poetic list of garden herbs gives us an idea of what would have been grown in the Tudor garden, along with their humours and uses.

Sweet rocket (*Hesperis matronalis*) is one of the traditional plants that would have flowered in early Tudor gardens (also known as damask violet, dame's violet, and dame's gillyflower).

of knowledge about culinary and medicinal herbs, but the Dissolution meant that it was the secular world that stepped forward to welcome, name and classify. Perhaps as a result of this there was less emphasis on the 'uses' that could be made of these new plants and instead a frisson of excitement over the possibilities for decoration and display. The most famous 'herbals' of the period, however, still searched hard to provide a *raison d'être* for each new discovery – one that would justify its existence in a world ordered by God for the better support of humankind. Advances in printing resulted in a series of such publications in the Tudor period, as well as the first coloured 'Florilegium', documenting the new arrivals as well as detailing variations on old favourites.

William Turner was the first to produce a 'herbal' in this period, written in the English language to reflect its non-monastic origins. Frustrated with the poor botanical tuition he had received at Cambridge in the 1530s ('where, as he could learn, [was] never one Greek, neither Latin nor English name, even amongst the Physicians, of any herb or tree'), Turner had compiled his own list of 238 plants. From this list sprang his *New Herball*, the first part of which was printed in 1551, although its second part was delayed by a further eleven years due to his religious exile on the continent.

This illustration, taken from Adam Lonicer's (1557) *Krauterbuch*, gives us an insight into the various raised bed planting and potted plants that might be expected in a sixteenth-century herbalist's or plant collector's garden. The genus *Lonicera* (honeysuckle) is named in Adam Lonicer's honour.

The title page
of John Gerard's
*Herball, Or Generall
Historie of Plantes*
(1597) illustrates
some of the
plants he
describes within
the book,
including the
'Crown Imperial',
maize, and fritillary.
Directly under
the date and
printer's name
are two red tulips.

To complete his work Turner drew both on his continental studies and on the gardens of his then patron and employer, the Duke of Somerset, at Syon, where Turner acted as combined chaplain and physician. Eventually becoming Dean of Wells Cathedral, Turner is now famously referred to as the 'father of English botany'. However, despite a diplomatic dedication to Queen Elizabeth, Turner's *New Herball* was to be superseded by the end of the century by the *Herball, or Generall Historie of Plantes* produced in 1597 by John Gerard, better known now by its colloquial title, 'Gerard's *Herball*'.

Gerard was at heart a gardener and plantsman who took pride in his own plant collection and that of his employer, the wealthy and horticulturally inclined William Cecil, Lord Burghley. In the 1590s Gerard compiled and printed a 24-page list of the plants in his own garden in London, and from this grew the much more comprehensive *Herball*; for this he drew on the gardens of plant-collecting friends including those of his employer at Theobalds (Hertfordshire) and the Strand, in London. Although Gerard included the medicinal use of plants, and names his work a 'herbal or general history', this was also a work that celebrated the new, the unusual and those plants noted for appearance rather than usage. In the completed book rarities and old favourites face each other across the pages, each carefully illustrated by woodcuts. Alongside notes on origin, uses, and hints on cultivation, months of sowing and flowering, and so on, were the names of those of his friends who grew these horticultural rarities. Of lily-of-the-valley, he remarks that there are two kinds: the first, which grew on Hampstead Heath (then 'four miles from London'), and the second – with a red flower – being 'a stranger in England: howbeit I have the same growing in my garden'. Of the more exotic sugar cane, Gerard remarks: 'Myself did plant some shoots thereof in my garden … but the coldness of our clymat made an end of mine'. Mixing with the lily-of-the-valley and the sugar cane in Gerard's London garden were the magnificent 'flower of the sun' (or sunflower), also known by Gerard as the 'Marigold of Peru'.

Gerard's entry for the fritillary, or chequered daffodil, notes that 'Of the facultie [use] of these pleasant floures there is nothing set downe in the antient or later Writer, but are greatly esteemed for the beautifying of our gardens, and the bosoms of the beautifull.'

By the late sixteenth century, the Americas, north and south, had begun to provide excitement and colour both to garden plot and plate with Turkey corn (maize), Indian cress (nasturtiums), and love apples (tomatoes), although of these only the nasturtium was countenanced as a profitable addition to English diets by Gerard. Maize was regarded as suitable only for swine feed or for 'barbarous Indians which know no better', and tomatoes as a cold fruit that yields 'very little nourishment to

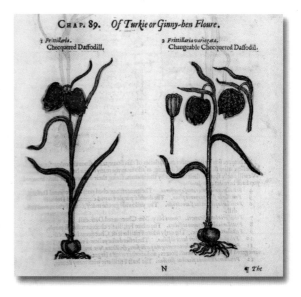

CHAP. 89.   *Of Turkie or Ginny-hen Floure.*

1 *Fritillaria.*
Cheequered Daffodill.

2 *Fritillaria variegata.*
Changeable Cheequered Daffodil.

14

the body, and the same naught and corrupt'. The 'henbane of Peru' – now rather better known as tobacco – was recommended as a panacea for aches and pains, either taken as syrup or inhaled. Tobacco flowers and leaves were also admired in the garden.

Opposite: Gerard noted that carnations and pinks were 'of such various colours and also severall shapes, that a great and large volume would not suffice to write of every one.' Names included Blunket, Horse-flesh, Gillofloure, Sops in Wine, Carnation, and Clove Gillofloure. Gerard himself had a rare 'yellow Gillofloure'.

Gerard's *Herball* provides us with one of the first records of potatoes in this country – named by him as 'Potato of Virginia ' – and also these splendid 'Apples of Love', better known nowadays as tomatoes!

Gerard's *Herball* is a useful catalogue of the plants available to the wealthier or more dedicated gardener by the end of the Tudor period, but the Tudors had always had a fascination with the new and the rare and most

Instantly recognisable from the woodcut illustration in Gerard's *Herball*, lavender was an essential component in Tudor gardens. Its grey leaves were popular for the creation of knots and it was also used for scent and colour in 'open knots'.

especially the edible. The royal gardens at Richmond, created by Henry VII, were noted in 1501 as having 'many vines, seeds and strange fruit, right goodly beset, kept and nourished with much labour and diligence'. Apricots, then known as 'apricocks', were also slowly spreading through England in the sixteenth century. Supposedly brought to England from Italy by Henry VIII's gardener in 1542, apricots were still little known in 1548 when William Turner published his *Names of Herbes*. By 1551 Turner noted 'many in Almany [Germany] and some in England'. In 1595 Shakespeare included a reference to apricots in his play *Richard II*, expecting his audience to understand (and incidentally introducing to the play an anachronism of fourteenth-century English apricots). Fruiting orange trees also made their appearance in the garden during the sixteenth century, courtesy of Sir Frances Carew of

3 *Lavendula minor,five Spica.*
Lauander Spike.

Beddington, Surrey, although Sir Francis is perhaps more famous for delaying the ripening of his cherry trees so that Queen Elizabeth I could be offered a freshly picked fruit on her visit in the late summer of 1599.

Not many Tudor gardens could boast of edibles from around the world, but by 1600 many were alive with the colours and scents of far-off countries extending both the variety and the season. The spring crocus (*Crocus vernus*) and the grape hyacinth (*Muscari botryoides*) arrived under the Tudors, as did the winter-flowering *Clematis cirrhosa* from southern Europe. For late spring the golden laburnum (*Lavandula anagyroides*) brightened gardens from *c.* 1560, whilst the lilac, the mock orange, the jasmine and the damask rose all combined to provide sweet scents in early summer. Toothed lavender (*L. dentata*) and *L. stoechas* (known by its common names 'stickadove' or French lavender) complemented the traditional *L. angustifolia* and *L. vera* – both useful in scented knot gardens.

It was not only botanists and herbalists who collected plants from abroad. Lord Edward la Zouche, diplomat and courtier, supposedly brought seeds of the 'thorn apple' (*Datura stramonium*) from Constantinople and donated them to friends and gardeners, including amongst them Gerard, who comments that he himself 'dispersed it through this land', as well as keeping some in his own garden. Strange looking as it is, the thorn apple was no match for the *Yucca gloriosa* or 'Spanish bayonet' that arrived in the 1550s. Notoriously difficult to flower except in warm climes, the creamy white bells caused a sensation when the plant finally flowered in the garden of Gerard's friend and fellow plantsman William Coys in 1604. Coys (1560–1627) also grew the sweet potato (*Ipomoea batatas*) and the persimmon (*Diospyros virginiana*) and his garden at Stubbers (Essex) must have been a showcase for plants from around the world. Courtiers and noblemen joined in the fashion for rare plants. In 1587 Francis Thynne noted that Cobham Hall (Kent) contained 'a rare garden … in which no varietie of strange flowers and trees do want, which praise or price maie obtaine from the furthest parts of Europe or from other strange Countries.'

The 'Apple of Peru' or thorn apple, supposedly introduced to England by Lord la Zouche.

The first full-colour florilegium was printed on the continent in 1590, and gave vivid colour to the new world of flowers. No longer needing the 'excuse' of medicinal or herbal uses, Adriaen Collaert's (1560–1618) *Florilegium* celebrated shape and colour, and reflected the wave of new collectors or 'florists' seeking out rarities and novelties. Ready to spark the fashion for such 'florists' flowers' in England, the 'Mountain Cowslip', 'Bear's ears' or, more properly, *Auricula*, was brought by Huguenots from France at the end of the sixteenth century. Over thirty varieties were known to Gerard. The African marigold (*Tagetes erecta*), the canna (*C. indica*), 'Marvel of Peru' (*Mirabilis jalapa*), hibiscus, 'Crown Imperial', and 'Busy Lizzie' (*Impatiens balsamina*) all thronged to add colour to the Tudor garden before the century was out.

But perhaps the brightest, shiniest, most colourful flower in the Tudor flower

1 *Stramonium Peregrinum.*
The Apple of Peru.

Corona Imperialis. **The Crowne Imperiall.**

The Crown Imperial in a (modern) coloured version of Gerard.

garden was the tulip. First spotted by European plant lovers in its native Turkey in the mid-sixteenth century, its fame spread rapidly – more rapidly than the plant itself, which was notoriously slow in its cycle from seed to flower. The first bulbs arrived in England in about 1578 from Constantinople via Austria, and although 'Tulipmania' did not take hold until the 1630s, their diverse colours added to the tapestry of the Tudor garden. Gerard called it 'a strange and forraine flower', but noted that it was one of several such flowers with which 'all studious and painfull herbarists desire to be better acquainted, because of that excellent diversitie of most brave flowers which it beareth.' Glorious though it was to look at, the tulip failed to compete with the traditional plants when it came to scent. Instead, as Shakespeare records, it was the violet, 'sweeter than the lids of Juno's eyes, or Cytherea's breath', which, along with thyme, lavender and the 'fragrant primrose', gave scent to the Tudor air. Flowers will not grow without some fertiliser and our visions of the sweetly scented Tudor garden may be brought back down to earth by this entry on manure in Thomas Hill's *The Gardener's Labyrinth*:

Doves dung is ye best, because the same possesseth a mightie hoteness. The dung also of the hen and other foules greatly commended for the sourness except ye dung of geese, duck and other waterfoules. A commendation next is attributed to the Asses dung, in that the same beast for his leisurely eating, digesteth easier and causeth the better dung. A third in place is the Goates dung, after this both the Oxe and Cow dung; next the Swines dung, worthier than the Oxen or Kine. The vilest and worst of all dungs … is the horse and moiles. The dung which men make (if the same be not mixed with the rubbich, or dust swept out of the house) is greatly mislyked, for that by nature it is hoter, and burneth the seedes sowne in the earth.

'GARDENS SO ENKNOTTED'

My garden sweet, enclosed with walles strong …
The knots so enknotted it cannot be espress't
With arbours and alyes so pleasant and so dulce.

William Cavendish, *c.* 1520, describing Hampton Court

ARTIFICE OF ALL KINDS was at the heart of the Tudor garden. In an era when few flowering plants outlasted the summer months, the garden was enlivened by patterns created from craftily woven herbs and evergreens, carpentry, and even paintwork. In Stephen Hawes' 1506 prose poem, *The Historie of Ground Amoure and La Bel Pucell, Called The Pastime of Pleasure*, the garden where the lovers met contained 'Flora paynted and wrought curiously, In diverse knottes of marveylous greatness'. In 1501 the royal gardens at Richmond also included:

'… royal knots, alleyed and herbed; [with] many marvelous beasts, as lions and dragons and such other diverse kinds, properly fashioned and carved in the ground, right well sounded and compassed in with lead.' Arbours and allées and carved figures gave an added dimension to the year-round garden, but it was the pattern of 'knots' that was the central theme. Varying over time, and between gardens, these might be simply a series of raised and hedged (or railed) beds laid parallel or at right angles to one another, forming patterns by their variation,

A design for a maze that might be made with various dwarf shrubs and herbs from Thomas Hill's *The Proffitable Arte of Gardening* (1568). The maze is a simple form of knot garden, using paths of chalk or sands for the contrast to the green.

23

This 'propre knot' is one of the most complicated, bearing much resemblance to embroidery. Hill remarks that it is suitable for planting in thyme or hyssop 'at the direction of the Gardener ... where as is spare room enough.'

This enclosed trellised garden with a relatively simple knot appears in Thomas Hill's *The Gardener's Labyrinth*.

or at the other end of the scale, elaborate and complex patterns of twining of herbs, evergreens, and flowers, often repeated over several beds, displaying the skill of the gardeners or the wealth of the owner.

A popular design was the 'quartered' garden of four knots. Such a 'quartered' garden, surrounded by fruit trees, was recommended in the rare gardening work, *A Short Instruction Verie Profitable and Necessarie for All Those that Delight in Gardening*, a 1591 English translation of a French book. Sanded walkways led between the knots, allowing the plants to be admired, whilst raised walkways,

terraces or mounds gave views of the patterns made by the plants. With the addition of a central feature in the knot garden, a fountain or basin, the knot garden (or gardens) was repeated endlessly in slightly differing forms and vastly differing scales up and down the country.

So ubiquitous was the patterned knot garden that almost all sixteenth- and seventeenth-century garden books contain designs for knots and advice on suitable plants with which to create them. Although many modern recreations have chosen the evergreen and easily maintained box to create knots, this was not a common choice in the Tudor period. In 1600 box was described by the writer Richard Surfleet as 'of naughtie smell' and was said to kill bees and 'corrupteth the aire', being an ill choice for the knot garden. Perhaps fortunately for Tudor bees, dwarf box was only just becoming available 'into the gardens of those that are curious' as late as 1629 according to John Parkinson. Instead, scented herbs were used to create the knots. Used in a variety of foliage colours and shapes these gave an extra 'dimension' to the twists and turns of the pattern. Santolina (cotton lavender), hyssop, thrift, germander, marjoram, savory, lavendar and thyme were all popularly recommended by authors such as Thomas Hill and John Parkinson. In his (1568) *Proffitable Arte of Gardening*, Hill described 'lavender cotton' as most commonly used, whereas Parkinson, writing in the early seventeenth century, records that thrift had been much favoured 'in the past'. Of the evergreens available in the period, juniper

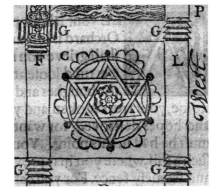

This Tudor Rose and Star knot design, set within a sunken garden, appeared as part of a larger garden design in William Lawson's *Country Housewife's Garden* (1618).

The 1594 version of Hill's 'propre knot' is a different, more geometric version.

The sunken knot garden at Hatfield House, one-time home of Elizabeth I. This knot garden was created by Lady (now Dowager Marchioness) Salisbury as a tribute to Robert Cecil, who built the present house in 1611. The present gardens have been created in box for year-round attractiveness.

and yew were thought to grow too quickly for use in a knot, as they would outgrow the pattern and overshadow the other plants.

Not all knot gardens contained flowers or even herbs. Some relied on white or yellow sands, chalks or gravels, or even red brick dust to create a contrast with the greens and greys of the knot. These artificial colours were also used to create pictorial 'knots' or heraldic arms. At Hampton Court a description by the traveller Thomas Platter in 1599 records: 'By the entrance I noticed numerous patches where square cavities had been scooped out, as for paving stones; some of these were filled with red brick-dust, some with white sand, and some with green lawn, very much resembling a chess board.'

The simplest knot gardens provided their pleasures by the patterns themselves, skilfully twisted and entwined in a variety of greens and greys, but others had an added dimension. In between the interwoven patterns could be planted a gay assortment of flowers of all colours, creating the

'jewelled' or tapestried effect so beloved of the period, although for much of the year the garden must have relied on the pattern of the knot and any carved or painted structures for its interest. In his *Herball*, Gerard envisaged 'the earth aparelled with plants in a robe of imbroidered works, set with orient pearles and garnished with great diversitie of costly jewels' – an appropriate analogy for a knot garden containing the latest rarities within its complex patterns, and here the bright colours of the new flowers from the Americas made their own contributions.

Larger gardens might contain numerous knots of differing patterns, or repeats of two or three patterns. In the 'Great Garden' at Theobalds (owned by William Cecil, Lord Burghley), we are told by a later visitor that 'there are nine large complete squares or knotts lying upon a levell in the middle of the said garden, whereof one is sett forth with box borders in the likeness of the Kinges armes …' His son Thomas' garden at Wimbledon was also recorded as having a 'Lower Level divided and cut into 4 great

The knot garden at the Garden Museum (London) was also designed by the Dowager Marchioness of Salisbury. It takes its inspiration from the work of the Elizabethan and Stuart plant collectors John Tradescant the Elder and Younger; many of the plants within the knot were grown by them.

Two of the four
knot gardens at
All Souls College,
Oxford, c. 1590.

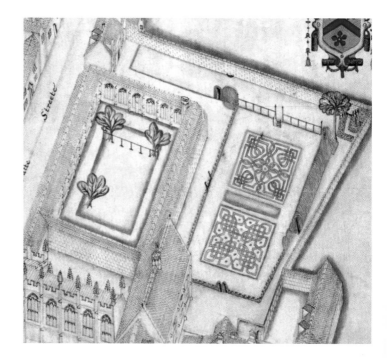

Herbs and box,
along with gravels,
have been used at
Otley Hall
(Suffolk) to
contrast the
design of the knot.

squares, the two middlemost whereof contain within them eight several squares, and well ordered knotts'. The inclusion of knots was expected of great gardens, so much so that in *Love's Labours Lost* (written in *c.* 1594) Shakespeare endows the King of Navarre with a 'curious knotted garden', although critics have often taken the comment and applied the symbol to the play itself with its twisting plot.

Although one might expect that the patterns became more intricate as the Tudor period went on, the designs printed in contemporary books suggest that this was not the case: some of the earliest patterns are the most complex. This leads us to query where the inspiration for the knot garden originated. The Tudors loved pattern in all forms of decorative and fine arts: carved woodwork in houses and churches, plasterers and pargetters,

The knot garden at the Tudor House and Garden (Southampton) was originally designed by the garden historian Dr Sylvia Landsberg. It has recently been restored using a wide range of plants and other materials popular in Tudor times.

glaziers and embroiderers, all used strap-work and knot-work motifs. The entwined initials of Henry VIII and Anne Boleyn were placed on the ceiling bosses of King's College Chapel, Cambridge, as well as picked out (less permanently) in embroidery and knots. Some knots had a 'meaning' (heraldic features or linked initials, or the classic 'lovers' knot', for example); others were simply pretty patterns.

Many of the knot patterns seen in gardening books appear to have their basis in embroideries. Thomas Hill's 'Propre Knot', variously illustrated in his *Proffitable Arte of Gardening* (1568 and later editions), appears almost too complex for anything but needle and thread. His knot recalls the twining decoration seen on clothes, bed hangings and even book covers. Francis Bacon, however, saw the likeness not to embroidery but to the intricate pastry patterns of tarts – and dismisses them as such. In 1618 William Lawson, in *The Countrie Housewife's Garden*, suggests that knot designs are 'as many as there are devices in gardener's braines ... The number of formes, mazes and knots is so great, and men are so diversely delighted, that I leave every House wife to herself.' At All Souls College, Oxford, one knot is supposed to have been based on the arms of the founder of the college, Archbishop Chichele (see page 28 illustration), whilst others appear to have been taken from Thomas Hill's *The Gardener's Labyrinth* (1577).

Below and pages 32–3: A combination of 'evergreens' herbs, sands and shell form the knot garden at Cressing Temple (Essex). The central planting feature adds height to the design.

Alongside knot patterns, gardening books also contained patterns for mazes or 'labyrinths', again made in hyssop, savory, thyme, lavender or marjoram. These were not the tall mazes described by a seventeenth-century writer as 'framed [to] a man's height', but low-hedged mazes, having much in common with the medieval religious 'footmaze', and created for the sake of the patterns they provided. Thomas Hill regarded both knots and mazes together as being 'for the comfort of the weary mind' and he may well have had in his own mind the religious symbolism attached to the maze as representing the journey of the good Christian through life. At Lyveden New Bield (Northamptonshire) the gardens of the Roman Catholic recusant, Thomas Tresham, contained a large foot maze, viewed from the four mounts set at each corner of the gardens. Often knots and mazes appeared together in gardens, the garden being first 'quartered' and then two mazes and two knots set out, and there appears to have been little distinction between the two, with the same plants being recommended for both.

Bur marigold (*Bidens cernua*) was one of the colourful flowers that visitors to Thomas Tresham's water gardens at Lyveden New Bield could admire.

This view of Lyveden New Bield (Northampton-shire) reveals the extent of the water features surrounding the main garden and curving around the mounts at each corner. The central maze has been reconstructed on the basis of a wartime aerial photograph taken by the Luftwaffe.

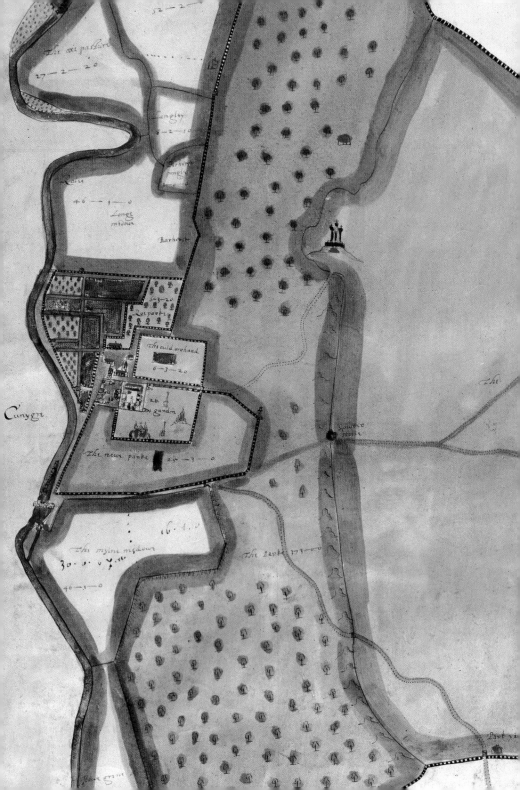

'A DULCET SPRING AND MARVAYLOUS FOUNTAINE'

One goes into the garden, encompassed with a ditch full of water, large enough to have the pleasure of going in a boat, and rowing between the shrubs …

Paul Hentzner, *Travels in England in the Reign of Elizabeth*, 1588

WATER delighted the Tudor garden visitor. Complex water gardens created patterns in the landscape, and kept animals from despoiling the carefully contrived gardens they enclosed, whilst the fish in the elaborate ponds and moats satisfied the dual purposes of entertainment and eating. As the Renaissance took hold, elaborate fountains spouted water and wine, although, as Francis Bacon pointed out, a still pool might mar all with its flies and frogs. Long associated with manor houses and castles, moats took on a new life in the Tudor period, joining with fishponds, lakes and all types of artificial waters to create a refreshing garden experience. In his work on gardens and estates of 1577, Barnaby Goodge included the suggestion that 'a little river with most cleare water, encompassing [a] garden doth wonderfully set it forth, and here withall the greene and goodly quickset hedge defendith it both from Man and Beest.'

Again royalty and courtiers led the way, equipped with sufficient money and the workforce to undertake the considerable earthworks, although even the wealthy looked to adapt existing features. At The More (Hertfordshire), Cardinal Thomas Wolsey, Chief Minister to Henry VIII and better known for his gardens at Hampton Court, based his water gardens on earlier moats around the site. For Thomas Tresham (1534–1605), courtier, politician and Catholic recusant, there were no such conveniences as an existing moat, and his large-scale hill-top water gardens at Lyveden New Bield commenced with the excavation of the four large inter-connecting ditches. Fed solely by rainfall, the moats surrounded the large circular maze, possibly laid out in turf or planted with fruit bushes and trees. Writing from the Bishop's Palace at Ely, where he was being held under house arrest, Tresham

Opposite:
The Tudor gardens at Chatsworth (shown here in a detail of the William Senior estate map of 1617) contained a water garden comprising a series of ponds with paths running between them. In the walled gardens were fountains and a further pond in 'the old orchard'.

instructed his surveyor, foreman and nurserymen on the construction of his new gardens with their four mounts beset by water. Recent investigation suggests that Elizabethan visitors would have rowed through the surrounding waters through colourful visions of fruit blossoms, pinks, bur marigold (*Bidens*), roses, strawberries, and herbs including coriander, parsley, and fennel.

Viewing gardens from the water appears to have been a popular Tudor pastime. The description at the head of the chapter is of the gardens of Theobalds, belonging to Lord Burghley, where boating was amongst the entertainments on offer to visitors by 1598. A ship or boat (presumably in stone) replete with 'cannon, flags and sails' also acted as a fountain, whilst more water spouted from a marble fountain to wet passers-by. In the wider park, Robert Cecil was busy creating a 'new river' after the death of his father. By the summer of 1601 the landscaper Adrian Gilbert reported that the river was 'better than if it were natural and has less impediments, more profit and [is] more beautiful.' In the immediate post-Elizabethan period Robert Cecil went on to create a diamond-shaped water parterre at Hatfield House, replete with islands, pavilions and water wheel. In the plan of the gardens two water monsters glide serenely between the banks.

Francis Bacon also created a 4-acre water garden at his family house of Gorhambury (Hertfordshire). Although not completed until after 1610, Bacon was making notes to himself (and memos to consult his cousin Robert Cecil) about the redesign of the existing 'Pond Yards' from much earlier. The pond gardens were located almost a mile from the actual house, taking advantage of the River Ver. A long avenue 'of most pleasant variegated verdure' connected the house and water garden. It might have been these ponds and basins that Bacon was thinking about when he wrote that '... water be never by rest discoloured green or red, or the like, or gather any mossiness or putrefaction' but should be in perpetual motion. The water gardens did not last long and by 1656 all that remained of them were ponds paved with coloured stones, and a supposed Roman banqueting house with black and white marble flooring. The rare 'Roman' house might have been inspired by Theobalds, where a summerhouse contained statues of twelve Roman emperors around an ornamental pool. Cisterns of lead set around the summerhouse contained fish, but were also used for bathing in summer. Again Bacon mentions such bathing facilities in his *Essay on Gardens*, and recommends lining them with coloured glass and images. Other Hertfordshire neighbours followed the fashion for water features, but it was not until after the death of Elizabeth and the close of the Tudor age that water gardens were created at nearby Ware Park, and at Bennington Park. The coloured stones in the ponds at Gorhambury recall the artificial fish

Rowing, or being rowed, at water level was a favourite pastime for Tudor garden visitors and revellers. Coloured stones and artificial fish added to the experience in some gardens.

The crescent-shaped lake at Elvetham (Hampshire), depicted here in 1591, was created for a single entertainment. The shape was perhaps suggested by Elizabeth's identification as the virgin goddess, Cynthia, often represented by a crescent moon. (From *The Honourable Entertainement given to the Queene Majestie in Progresse, at Elvetham, Hampshire*).

described in the water garden of Beddington (Surrey) belonging to Sir Francis Carew. Probably made for the visit of Elizabeth in 1599, a later visitor recorded the crystal clear water with plants and 'neatly made fishes, frogs etc. swimming … as if they were alive.'

Perhaps the most inventive of water gardens was that created at Elvetham (Hampshire) for the entertainment of Elizabeth I on her visit to the owner, the Earl of Hertford, in September 1591. Inspired by the defeat of the Spanish Armada in 1588, the Earl created a crescent-shaped lake within which were three islands: one in the shape of a ship; another a 'snail mount'; the third a fort, complete with turrets. The 'snail-mount' took on the role of slow Spain, whilst the ship engaged in battle on the lake. Elizabeth sat enthroned at the edge of the lake and sea gods arose from the 'deeps' to celebrate her triumphs. Used for only one entertainment, the lake was then abandoned. Similar entertainments were staged in the lakes and meres surrounding the castle at Kenilworth (Warwickshire) during Elizabeth's visit to the site, and many a chain of medieval fishponds must have been hastily altered to create a more aristocratic water feature on news of the court's intended visits. After Elizabeth's symbolic linkage with the goddess Venus-Virgo, water became even more essential to any royal celebration.

Smaller water gardens were often associated with manor houses of the gentry, again often adapted from earlier features. Examples exist as earthworks at sites such as Kettleby (Lincolnshire), Alderton (Northamptonshire), and Eltisely (Cambridgeshire). Other garden sites were merely moated, rather than boasting more complex water features, such as the late Tudor / Jacobean site at Shelley (Suffolk).

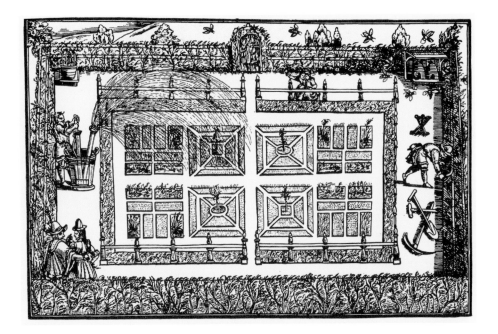

Water did not merely enclose Tudor gardens: it also splashed and spouted from fountains and ponds. In 1509 Stephen Hawes envisaged a garden, perhaps based on Henry VII's Richmond, where:

> In the myddle there was resplendes haunte
> A dulcet spring and marvaylous fountaine
> Of golde and asure made all certaine.

To the early Tudors, for whom hydraulics were largely unfamiliar, fountains were nothing short of a miracle. Basic pumping devices were known (including hand pumps) and could be used to water gardens for more practical purposes, but only the best-travelled had seen the fantastic fountains at gardens such as the Villa d'Este and the first description of these gardens in English was not published until 1594. Even by 1660 the famous diarist Samuel Pepys struggled to describe the classical 'Archimedes screw' that was being used to lift water from the Thames to the new water features in St James' Park. He resorted to images of 'one round thing going within all with a pair of stairs round; which being laid at an angle of 45 doth carry up the water with a great deal of ease.'

During most of the sixteenth century even the most resplendent of fountains were firmly architectural and the water little more than a

In the absence of engines to pump water, gardeners would pump by hand for practical purposes. This image is from Thomas Hill and provides a rather optimistic view of the distance and height that might be obtained from a small water tub pump.

downward dribble. Often octagonal, they rose in tiers, sometimes with a canopy, or were topped with a heraldic creature. Water dripped or dribbled, perhaps occasionally gushed, through animal heads, or very occasionally parts of human anatomy. The best-known image of a Tudor fountain is not strictly speaking a garden fountain, but that at the Field of Cloth of Gold, that resplendent coming together of the kings of France and England. Spouting wine

The recreated Tudor fountain at the Cressing Temple Tudor Garden, with spouts in the form of the 'Green Man'. The gardens also include raised viewing platforms for admiring the knot patterns and culinary herbs. An arbour is planted with woodbine, roses and oxlips.

for the duration of the celebrations, the fountain was topped by a figure of Bacchus. Anthony van Wyngaerde's image of Whitehall Palace in the mid-sixteenth century depicts a similar fountain, although presumably by then spouting water, and the recent recreation of Henry VIII's gardens at Hampton Court has been joined by a 13-foot-high replica of the 'Field of Cloth of Gold' fountain, created in timber, lead, bronze and gold leaf in the courtyard.

Architectural scale and detail were the hallmark of royal Tudor garden fountains, rather than quantity of water (or wine). At Windsor, Queen Mary installed a 30-foot-high fountain with an ornamental frieze, lead canopy and heraldic animals. A lion and eagle, 6 feet tall, crowned the fountain, holding 'a great vane with the royal arms of England and Spain' commemorating her marriage to Philip of Spain. Her half-sister Elizabeth may have been attempting to better her when she commissioned a 'very bewtifull fountain' at Hampton Court, at 'great charge' in 1590. White marble and coloured stonework was used, topped by a glittering figure of Justice – perhaps an odd choice for a fountain. The actual water flowed through the figure of an 'antikeboy', although from which part of him is not specified. These 'antikeboys' were to reappear as 'pissing boy' fountains at Bolsover (Derbyshire) in the seventeenth century; and in a rare 'pissing men' basin or pond, for which we have only the design by John Smythson. For the visit of Elizabeth I to their Suffolk manor house, the Drury family invested in a combined statue/fountain with a very similar motif. The statue, in the shape of a Hercules or 'Green Man', is a superb amalgamation of medieval English and Renaissance European, and welcomed the Virgin Queen by issuing water from his manly parts.

At Kenilworth (Warwickshire), Robert Dudley, Earl of Leicester, created a more recognisably classical fountain. At the base an octagonal basin of fine white alabaster (decorated with scenes from Ovid's *Metamorphoses*) contained fish; according to a visitor, 'wherein pleasantly playing to and fro carp, tench, bream and for varietie pearch and eel'. From the centre of the basin rose a column with two Athlants holding aloft between them a globe, from whence piped water dropped into the basin below. The description continues: from this 'fayr formed boll of a three foot over: from wheans sundry fine pipez did lively distill continuall streamz intoo the receyt of the Foountayn'. All were topped by a Ragged Staff – heraldic emblem of the Earls of Leicester – as again Tudor England went head to head with the classical world. Classical statues were rare in Tudor gardens, but were certainly increasingly regarded as something to aspire to: in the Countess of Pembroke's *New Arcadia* (1590/8) the imagined garden contained, 'A naked Venus of white

Two of the remarkable 'pissing boy' statues on the fountain at Bolsover (Derbyshire).

marble, wherein the grauer had vsed such cunning, that the naturall blew veines of the marble were framed in fitte places, to set foorth the beautifull veines of her bodie.' No wonder that in gardens such as this water was also arranged to spout out at unwary visitors whose desires might be inflamed by such sights.

This rare example of a surviving Elizabethan statue/fountain greeted Elizabeth I on her visit to the Drury family of Suffolk in 1578. 'Pissing men' and 'pissing boys' were popular in the late sixteenth and early seventeenth centuries, as also evidenced by the surviving fountain and bathing pool at Bolsover Castle, Derbyshire.

Recreated by English Heritage in the gardens at Kenilworth (Warwickshire), the Athlants fountain astounded the court in the summer of 1575. Robert Langham recorded that visitors 'inflamed' by the images from Ovid, were cooled by water 'spurting upward with such vehemency, as they should ... be moistened from top to toe.'

'ALL MANNER OF CARPENTERS' WORK'

They have gardens ... with their harbers and bowers fit for the purpose.
And least they might be espied in these open places they have their banquetting
houses with galleries, turrets and what not, therein sumptuously erected;
wherein they may (and doubtless do) many of them play the filthy persons ...

Phillip Stubbes, *Anatomie of Abuses in England* (1583)

FROM THE MOST ELABORATE of banqueting towers to the most basic of treehouses, garden structures of all kinds delighted the Tudors, whether intent on privacy or dalliance. Allées and galleries, often covered with winding plants for shade and shelter, criss-crossed the gardens, with 'windows' cut to allow views out, or glimpses into the enclosed garden areas. These long walks echoed the idea of the 'long gallery' inside the house, used by women and men alike for private talks as well as exercise. In Shakespeare's *Much Ado About Nothing*, a play where much of the action is set in a garden, Hero and Leander talk loudly of Benedict's love for Beatrice whilst walking in the garden allées, knowing that Beatrice can overhear them from her hidden bower – a bower 'Where honeysuckles, ripened by the sun, forbid the sun to enter', and a maiden may keep her complexion. Such allées, covered and uncovered, may be seen on countless images of European gardens in this period, although sadly we have to be content with mere descriptions for English Tudor allées. In 1577, Thomas Hill declared:

> ... [allées] serve to good purposes, the one is that the owner may diligently view the properties of his herbes and flowers, the other for the delight and comfort of his wearied mind, which he may by himself or in fellowship of friendes conceyve in the delectable sightes and fragrant smelles of the flowers.

An early description of the gardens of Henry VII at Richmond (Surrey) includes reference to 'raised galleries' from which the gardens might be seen, and, within

Opposite:
The solitary banqueting house at Melford Hall (Suffolk) conforms to Tudor design, in its two storeys with separate entrances and the positioning to look into and out of the garden.

45

Right: A covered allee with 'carpenters' work' recreates the feel of a sixteenth-century garden.

Far right: One of a pair of magnificent bowers that flank the terrace in the recreated gardens at Kenilworth (Warwickshire). Painted, gilded and covered with honeysuckle and eglantine roses, these would have shaded the face of the Virgin Queen.

This raised and covered area shown in Thomas Hill's *The Gardener's Labyrinth* appears to be a cross between a raised gallery and a bower. Covered in vines, it would have shaded its occupants from the fierce sun shown to the right!

the gardens, 'housis of plesure to disporte in'. At Thornbury, a 'privy' (or private) garden could also be seen from a raised gallery, whilst recent research at Lambeth Palace suggests that a long gallery atop a loggia extended from the palace itself out into the gardens. These 'garden galleries' allowed gardens to be accessed under shelter, often direct from the private quarters of the main house, and gave fine views over the various knots and patterns. At Windsor, Queen Elizabeth I added a long terrace and gallery just below the privy lodgings, and Henry Hawthorne, Purveyor of the Queen's Works, was instructed to create 'perfect plattes' for the gallery and banqueting house.

Mounts gave further opportunity to gaze, both out and down, on the patterned garden or the wilder landscapes beyond. Earthen mounts were usually created on the outer corners of gardens, although occasionally examples were placed centrally. To help people reach the top, mounts were often created with encircling paths, which gave them the appearance of a snail shell – hence their name, 'snail-mounts'. In 1540 John Leland

This image of a wooden covered pavilion dates to c. 1600 and clearly shows the popularity of such 'summerhouses' for entertaining.

One of the two snail-mounts at the Elizabethan garden at Lyveden New Bield. A path still leads to the top.

described the mount at Wressell Park (East Riding) as 'writhen about with turnings of cokilshells to come to the top without payne'. Perhaps the largest and best-recorded snail-mound was that at Hampton Court, which by Henry VIII's time was topped by the fabulous onion-domed banqueting house with its glittering glass windows. A series of mounts still survives at the symbolic gardens of Lyveden New Bield: two of a pyramidal shape and two 'snail-mounts' complete with paths. A remarkably similar conical snail-mount is clearly shown in the background of Robert Peake's 1603 portrait of Princess Elizabeth, daughter of James I, in this case topped by a treehouse.

Treehouses provided a way in which to appreciate the patterns within Tudor gardens, as well as views out to surrounding deer parks. Some were even sited within the park, overlapping in function with viewing towers. Often elaborately constructed, with ramps, stairs, and multi-level galleries, treehouses appear to have spread from the classical world, through the great Renaissance gardens of Italy, and north to the low countries and England. There are no known descriptions of specific treehouses in Tudor gardens, but the scale of those described by early Stuart commentators suggests they were well established by the early seventeenth century. Writing in 1629, John Parkinson described the treehouses at Cobham Hall (Kent):

> ... a tall or great bodied Line [lime] tree, bare without boughes for eight foote high, and then the branches were spread round about so orderly ... and brought to compasse that middle Arbour: And from those boughes the

body was bare againe for eight or nine foote (wherein might bee placed halfe an hundred men at the least, as there might be likewise in that underneath this) & then another rowe of branches to encompasse a third arbour ....

Stairs joined the various levels at Cobham, whilst simpler ladders might give access to smaller tree galleries or houses.

Frequently encountered in medieval gardens, and carrying on into Tudor gardens, were other temporary garden structures such as arbours, bowers, and pavilions. In *The English Husbandman* (1613) Gervase Markham declared that 'arbours and Summer-bowers to feast in' were so common that 'every labourer can make them'. 'Carpenter's work' (as it was known) both framed gardens and divided them, and provided shelter both to plant

The garden in the background of this portrait of Princess Elizabeth (daughter of James I) has not been positively identified, although Elizabeth was under the guardianship of Lord Harrington at Coombe Abbey (Warwickshire). It may be an imaginary backdrop, incorporating fashionable features including water gardens, mount and a treehouse/pavilion.

The herber in a Garden may bee framed with Juniper poles, or the Willowe, eyter to stretch, or be bound together with Osyers, after a square forme, or in arche manner winded, that the braunches of the Vine, Melon or Cucumbre, running and spreading all over, might so shadowe and keepe both the heate and Sunne from the walkers and sitters thereunder.

Thomas Hill, *The Gardener's Labyrinth*, 1577

The modern snail-mount at the Tudor gardens at Otley Hall (Suffolk). Adults take the official path down whilst children simply roll.

and person. Tents and pavilions could be used to make 'instant gardens', most popular for visits of royalty. The large garden and landscape created at Elvetham (Hampshire) for the visit of Queen Elizabeth in 1591 included many such pavilions, and 'a withdrawing place for her Majestie', with 'walls cover'd with boughs, and clusters of ripe hasell nuttes, the inside with arras, the roofe of the place with works of ivy leaves, the floor with sweet herbes and green rushes'. At Whitehall Palace, Elizabeth herself commissioned a banqueting house of birch boughs and ivy beneath a roof of canvas. Painted and gilded canvas permitted an array of 'mock' buildings and even *trompe-l'oeil* landscapes. In 1577 Barnaby Goodge remarked that by using tapestries, one might:

bedeck … your parlers and your banqueting houses both within and without … with pictures of beautiful flowres and trees, that you may not only feed your eyes with the beholding of the true and lively flowre, but also delight your selfe with the counterfaite in the middest of Winter.

At Nonsuch Palace (Surrey) Henry VIII created a single 'great' banqueting house, again raised on a mount, with balconies around, whilst twelve lesser 'arbours' dotted the grounds, most probably more temporary structures. Turning the fashion for temporary pavilions into something more permanent, Henry VIII created a series of arbours and banqueting houses in his gardens at Hampton Court Palace. The most magnificent of these was the 'great round arbour', started in 1533. Three storeys high, richly and ornately glazed, gilded and painted, the brick-built arbour sat atop a tall mount overlooking the complex of knot gardens and the River Thames. If the 'great arbour' happened to be full then there was a wide choice of other retreats. Referred to in the royal accounts variously as 'banket houses' and 'arbours', there were five more in the Tilt Yard gardens alone, plus extras in the Privy Garden, and others liberally inserted into walls and odd corners, many resembling tall towers rather than the more squat, two-storey form later associated with the term 'banqueting house'. As their name implies, 'banqueting' or 'banking' houses were used as part of the complex feasting entertainments in the Tudor period, but not for the whole of the feast. Banqueting houses, with their fine views but limited cooking facilities, were used for the consumption of the often finely wrought sweet courses. Coloured marzipans in all shapes and guises, playing cards made of sugars, and spiced and mulled wines were favourites.

Themselves probably triggered by European fashion, Henry VIII's garden buildings at Hampton Court led the way for a rush of English examples. The fashion for matching pairs of banqueting houses appears to have started in the 1530s, and examples from the first part of the sixteenth century still survive today at Hales Place, Tenterden (Kent), Roydon Hall (Kent), and Montacute House (Somerset), whilst single examples can be seen at Melford Hall (Suffolk), and Sissinghurst (Kent). The Sissinghurst example has been heavily modified over time, and is now known as 'The Priest's House', but began life in the mid-sixteenth century as a garden pavilion or banqueting house, in which guise it may have entertained Queen Mary on her visit in 1557, or Queen Elizabeth in 1573. Ashby de la Zouch (Leicestershire) had three brick-built garden houses, each of a different design. A tall 'clover leaf' tower at one end of a raised terrace was 'mis-matched' by an octagonal version at the other end. Recently discovered by excavation (in 2006) was a third summerhouse in the centre of the unusual earthwork gardens, again dating to the period 1500–50. The gardens at Ashby de la Zouch may also

The 'cloverleaf' plan banqueting house at Ashby de la Zouch was one of three banqueting houses within the garden: two at either end of the raised terrace, and the third in the centre of the earthwork garden. From the upper levels one could have looked down on the complex gardens or out into the wider designed landscape.

have contained a patterned gardened laid out with coloured stones. In 1613 Gervase Markham suggested that, in general, 'Some curious and artificial banqueting house … would give lustre to the Orchard', and five years later William Lawson recommended that such pavilions should be set at either end of a garden, on a mount or other raised walk, reflecting recent fashions.

Single banqueting houses or pavilions did exist, and indeed may have become more popular in the later sixteenth century. William Cecil placed a central building in his 85-square-foot sunken garden at Wimbledon (Surrey), probably between 1588 and 1603, and also complemented his paired garden buildings at the Strand (London) with a further central building, recalling the three banqueting houses at Ashby de la Zouch. Perhaps most evocatively, Elizabeth I had a banqueting pavilion built beside the Thames at Whitehall, where 'The ceiling painted with clouds, sun and stars, had baskets depending from it full of fruit spangled with gold.' This painted banqueting house recalls again the fictional garden in the Countess of Pembroke's *Arcadia*: 'Hard by was a house of pleasure builte for a Sommer retiring place, where Kalander leading him, he found a square roome full of delightfull pictures, made by the most excellent workeman of Greece.' Set in a mythical classical past, the *Arcadia* drew on fashionable gardens of England and suggests that interior decoration was sought after in summerhouses, as with banqueting houses.

ROYALTY AND PAGEANT

ROYAL GARDENS set the trends that courtiers followed. For the Tudors, the numerous royal palaces provided opportunities for display of both status and fashion. Under Henry VII the gardens at Richmond combined pleasure with power, whilst the royal gardens of Henry VIII reflected the 'pleasure seeking' and ostentation for which his reign was famous. Glittering glass façades and gilded carpenters' work demonstrated to everyone his grip on his own treasury, and his famous rivalry with the French kings. Elizabeth was more cautious over her own funds, but delighted to inspire gardening ambition in others through her frequent courtly progressions. Paintings, plans and descriptions give an insight into these gardens of power over the twelve decades of Tudor reign and bring together our vision of the different features found in Tudor gardens.

Richmond Palace (Surrey) is the best known of Henry VII's gardens and was his favourite palace. Most probably elaborated for the marriage of his son Arthur, Prince of Wales, to Catherine of Aragon in 1501, the gardens contained 'royal knots', allées, orchards and bowling greens, as well as 'pleasant galleries and houses of pleasure to disport in, at chess tables, dice,

Paintings of the royal gardens are rare, but we can glimpse the gardens of Whitehall Palace through the archways in the painting *The Family of Henry VIII*, c. 1545 (artist unknown). Raised beds are defined by painted rails of white and green, and set within these are painted posts topped with heraldic figures.

cards and billiards'. The sporting component, perhaps emphasised for the occasion of the wedding, also included bowling alleys, archery butts, and 'tennis plays', to amuse both those who themselves disported and those who 'behold them so disporting'. In addition to the human occupants of the garden we are told there were 'many marvellous beasts, as lions, dragons and such other of divers kinds, properly fashioned and carved in the ground, right well sounded and compassed in with lead' – in other words a heraldic knot garden. Unfortunately, later drawings of the gardens and palace do not show these heraldic knots, although they do show a 'foot-maze' or labyrinth.

Henry VIII may have taken his inspiration from his father, but perhaps more influential was the competition with his arch-rival Francis I. By the time the two kings met on the Field of the Cloth of Gold in 1520, Francis was already creating some of the most magnificent gardens ever seen in northern Europe, most notably at the Château of Blois and, from 1519 onwards, Château Chambord. With its extensive symmetrical Renaissance-style gardens, galleries and covered allées, Blois was to become the touchstone against which Henry was to match himself in his gardens at Whitehall and Hampton Court. Henry still had one fashionable foot firmly in the heraldic past of Tudor England, and so his gardens never attained the symmetrical perfection of the European kings but were instead filled with an array of buildings, sundials and heraldic beasts in glorious, gaudy colour.

A heraldic beast at the recreated Tudor Gardens at Southampton.

Whitehall Palace, taken from Cardinal Wolsey in 1529, was spread over 23 acres. Within that a privy garden of some 120 metres by 75 metres contained raised beds of red brick, with planting retained by wooden rails in green and white. In the centre of the garden was a large, triple-storeyed 'trickle-fountain', which contemporary descriptions tell us combined with a sundial. Perhaps most startling to modern eyes would be the splendid heraldic beasts, lavishly gilded and each grasping a small flag, set on posts in the gardens.

Heraldic beasts appeared again at Hampton Court, this time in both the depiction of the gardens and the royal accounts. In 1534 the King's accounts record that an Edward More (of Kingston) was paid 20 shillings apiece for carving 159 of the 'kinges beastes', whilst other entries in the accounts refer to the making of lions, greyhounds, dragons, hinds, antelopes, griffins, leopards, tigers, harts and badgers – some of which bore 'shieldes with the kinges arms and the queen's'. Some at least of this astounding array of figures appear in the Wyngaerde sketch of Hampton Court, standing around the compartmented gardens like anti-social garden visitors, each carefully spaced from the next. A similar arrangement of beasts can also be discerned in Wyngaerde's drawing of the Whitehall Palace. Leopold van Wedel, who visited the gardens of Whitehall in 1584, describes thirty-four heraldic beasts, holding aloft vanes with the queen's arms, so even if the beasts themselves were left over from the reign of her father, Elizabeth had presumably changed the arms. King Henry's accounts for Hampton Court also record the painting of hundreds of yards of rails, presumably to surround the raised beds as at Whitehall.

As well as the carved beasts more figures dotted the gardens. In 1599 a German visitor recorded that there were:

> … all manner of shapes [made from plants]. Men, women, centaurs, sirens, serving maids with baskets, delicate crenellations etc. – all made from dry twigs bound together and green quick-set shrubs and rosemary, all true to life and so cleverly and amusingly interwoven, mingled and grown together, trimmed and arranged.

A rare surviving polyhedral sundial of the type that would have astounded the visitors to the royal Tudor gardens. Madeley Court, near Telford, Shropshire.

Sundials, a remarkable scientific 'curiosity' in the sixteenth century, also took their place in the crowded royal gardens. Henry VIII had sixteen sundials placed around the gardens and walls of Hampton Court and by the reign of Queen Elizabeth a 'remarkable sundial showing the time in thirty different ways' stood in the Privy Garden in Whitehall. Rather unusually it apparently also had the ability to squirt water at persons looking at it. This sundial was described again in the 1620s by the Duke of Saxony who recorded that it was 'a great quadrangular stone, hollow in the middle and round like a baptismal fount . . . [with] over 117 sun circles on which you can see the hours.' It also recorded the zodiac and the months, turning the royal garden into a home for the burgeoning Renaissance sciences.

Elizabeth followed but never matched her father in the royal gardens. Descriptions of Elizabeth's own palace gardens strike a slightly old-fashioned chord with their beasts and woven serving maids, and although she was celebrated as the goddess of spring and the 'virgin rose', Elizabeth appears to have let others undertake the expense of fashionable garden creation. Royal progresses (popularised to take the

The recreated
aviary at
Kenilworth takes
pride of place in
the gardens, facing
the terraced walk.
Once again the
gardens are filled
with bird song,
as they were
for the visit of
Queen Elizabeth I.

court away from London in the heat and disease of summer) demanded garden entertainments and entire landscapes were created to satisfy the demand for pageantry and performance encouraging her courtiers to court the queen in flowers. Scented privy gardens sprang up to greet Elizabeth, lakes were created overnight for elaborate water pageants, and classical statues from the continent ousted traditional heraldic figures in an attempt to impress. Weeks of entertainments, poetry, and dances were planned for garden and house, including performances of Shakespeare's latest plays. Gardens such as Kenilworth (Warwickshire), Theobalds (Hertfordshire), Wimbledon (Surrey), Nonsuch (Surrey), Wollaton Hall (Nottinghamshire), Audley End (Essex), Holdenby House (Northamptonshire), and Cobham Hall (Kent) were all 'encreast by occasion of her Majesty's often coming', or at the very least by the expectation of her coming, whilst others such as Kirby Hall (Northamptonshire) were caught up in the general fashion of garden making.

To Flora
E mpresse of flowers, tell where away
L ies your sweet Court this merry May,
I n Greenewich garden allies?
S ince there the heavenly powers do play
A nd haunt no other vallies
...
R oses and lilies did them draw,
E re they divine Astraea saw;
G ay flowers they sought for pleasure:
I nstead of gathering crownes of flowers,
N ow gather they Astrea's dowers,
A nd beare to heaven their treasure.

John Davies, Hymn IX, *Hymnes to Astraea*, 1600.

The piece is written as an acrostic, the first letters of the full verses spelling out Elisabetha Regina.

Going all out to impress, Robert Dudley, Earl of Leicester, was one of those who created an entirely new garden. For the visit of Elizabeth to Kenilworth (Warwickshire) in 1575 (and perhaps the earlier visit in 1565) he created a garden, 'Beautified with many delectable, fresh and umbragioous bowers, arbez and seats and walks, that with great art, cost and diligens wear very pleasantlie appointed'. Occupying an acre and overlooked by a terraced walk, the garden comprised four quarters set with jewel-like flowers, with paths in-between of fine sand. In the centre of each quarter were obelisks of purple porphyry, whilst in the centre of the garden was a marble fountain in Renaissance, rather than Tudor, style, comprised of two 'Athlants' figures holding aloft a globe. Harking back to the heraldic figures of Henry VIII were the prominent carved 'Bear and Ragged Staff' figures, which represented Dudley in his guise as Earl of Leicester.

Decorated with artificial sapphires, rubies and diamonds, the aviary also has the gilded initials of Robert [Earl of] Leicester.

Kenilworth's gardens were described in detail by an astounded courtier, Robert Langham, whose only weakness as a garden 'commentator' was that he obviously did not know the names of the flowers and plants that Leicester had used, referring only to 'the sweetness of savour on all sides, made so respirant from the redolent plants and fragrant herbs and flowers, in form, colour, and quantity so deliciously variant; and fruit-trees bedecked with apples, pears, and ripe cherries.' This last claim at least may be regarded as an exaggeration, given that the visit took place in July, when most apples and pears are still only tiny fruits. An aviary with arcaded 'windows', decorated in 'sapphires, rubies and diamonds' contained exotic birds to entertain eye and ear. Or in the words of Langham:

> Birds, English, French, Spanish, Canarian, and I am deceived if I saw not some African. Whereby, whether it became more delightsome in change of tunes, and harmony to the ear; or else in difference of colours, kinds, and properties to the eye, I'll tell you, if I can, when I have better bethought me.

The fabulous gardens at Theobalds (Hertfordshire), a convenient day's travel from London, were also in part created for the reception of Elizabeth's court on their summer revels, and played host to Elizabeth numerous times. Owned by that indefatigable garden creator, William Cecil, Lord Burghley, with the aid of the herbalist John Gerard, these were divided between the Privy Garden and the Great Garden. The Privy Garden, complete with knots and planted with tulips, lilies and peonies, with round arbours at the corners, raised walkways, and twenty-eight cherry trees, was out of bounds to most visitors and our earliest description comes from 1650, by which time the house itself was in royal hands. However, the Great Garden, covering over 7 acres, was documented by a visitor in 1598 (the same year the gardens were inherited by Cecil's son Robert). Divided into nine 'knots' of 70 feet square, with a central white marble fountain, these must have born resemblance to Kenilworth, at least in layout. The knots were planted with 'choice flowers', whilst two contained figures of 'wild men' created from 'wainscott well carved'. In 1610–11 the hands and feet of these wild men were painted (or re-painted) in 'carnation colour' oil paint (presumably a flesh colour). An armorial knot also had carved additions recorded in an account book, 'for cutting and carving two great heads four handles and four feet for the supporters of the Queen's Armes ... in a knot in the garden'. Elizabeth was also present in the form of a 'Venusberg' mount and labyrinth, perhaps left over from some entertainment at one of her visits. Canals, fruit trees, and a loggia painted with the genealogy of the Cecils completed the garden, whose scale and magnificence far exceeded any other Tudor garden, as befitted Elizabeth's Secretary of State. So magnificent was it that when James I came to the throne he too favoured the house and gardens with frequent visits, and in 1607 'acquired' the house and gardens from Robert Cecil in exchange for the nearby Hatfield House. Thomas Cecil, older brother of Robert, also created gardens at his property in Wimbledon (Surrey). Again a Privy Garden and a Great Garden divided the court and the common visitors; again four open knots set around a fountain decorated the Privy Garden, whilst in the Great Garden the open knots had at their centre a pillar. The pillar was a 'device' associated with Elizabeth who took the emblem from the famous 'Pillars of Hercules' *impresa* of Emperor Charles V following her own triumph over the Spanish Armada in 1588. Herb gardens, formal orchards, and a banqueting house set within a sunken garden all added to the attractions at Wimbledon, and it is no surprise that the queen visited four times between 1592 and 1602, despite her own increasing age.

Nonsuch Palace, as portrayed by John Speed in his 1610 *Survey of Surrey*. Only a very small area of the gardens can be seen, including the columns topped by the Lumley Popinjays and a central fountain.

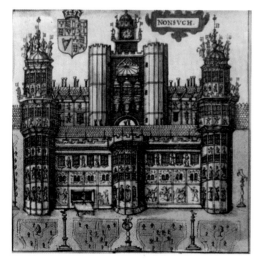

In the late Tudor garden royal symbolism gradually moved away from traditional heraldry, with its outlandish beasts and naming puns, and turned instead towards the classical and the Renaissance. To the Tudor Rose of her father, and the Falcon of her mother, Elizabeth increasingly added (or had added for her) an array of classical allusions: identified after the Armada sea battle as the sea-born Venus-Virgo, the moon-goddess Cynthia (who controls the waves), she also took on the guise of the virginal Diana the Huntress, and Astraea–Virgo the goddess of perpetual spring. Added to these personifications were classical emblems such as the Pillars of Hercules, the sieve or riddle of the wise virgin Tuccia, the phoenix of rebirth and chastity, and the pelican plucking out its heart to feed its young, symbol of Elizabeth's motherhood to the nation. Scholarly courtiers picked up on the symbolism, adding it into poetry, painting and of course gardening – such as Robert Cecil's 'Venusberg', or the central Pillar at Wimbledon. Perhaps the most important symbolic garden of the period was that of Nonsuch Palace (Surrey). Built by Henry VIII, by 1579 it was in possession of John, Lord Lumley. A Roman Catholic, excluded from court and office, Lumley was well versed in classical symbolism, having travelled in Catholic Italy. Between c. 1579 and 1591 Lumley created a unique garden. Amongst the knots and embroidered plants were statues, marble basins and fountains, water jets, wilderness walks, grotto and groves. In homage to his queen a Diana fountain splashed water into a marble basin, whilst a further fountain was topped by a crescent moon and crown. A Diana grove contained springs of water and a tableau telling the story of the folly of Actaeon and his hounds. In the Privy Garden tall columns supported the Lumley family's symbol, the Popinjay, but in addition a marble wash basin was crowned with a regal Pelican. In other parts of the ground a Temple of Diana, pyramids, and more columns or pillars supported carved eagles, pelican and phoenix. Nonsuch was a garden where Tudor past met Renaissance future, and Renaissance triumphed.

This model of Nonsuch Palace, created by Ben Taggart for the Friends of Nonsuch and based on the research of Professor Martin Biddle, includes detail of the gardens.

GARDENS AND MUSEUMS TO VISIT

Ashby de la Zouch Castle, South Street, Ashby-de-la-Zouch, Leicestershire
LE65 1BR. Telephone: 01530 413343.
Website: www.english-heritage.org.uk
Ruined castle with unique Tudor garden earthworks.

Charlecote Park, Wellesbourne, Warwick CV35 9ER.
Telephone: 01789 470277.
Website: wwww.nationaltrust.org.uk/charlecote-park
Tudor house and deer park, supposedly visited by Shakespeare.

Cressing Temple Tudor Garden, Witham Road, Cressing, Braintree, Essex CM77
8PD. Telephone: 01376 584903.
Website: www.cressingtemple.co.uk
Recreated Tudor walled garden, complete with water spouts, raised
platform and physic garden.

Garden Museum, 5 Lambeth Palace Road, London SE1 7LB.
Telephone: 020 7401 8865.
Website: www.gardenmuseum.org.uk
Collections of images, books and objects and a knot garden.

Hampton Court Palace, East Molesey, Surrey KT8 9AU.
Telephone: 0844 482 7777.
Website: www.hrp.org.uk/HamptonCourtPalace
Tudor Palace and recreated Tudor gardens with heraldic beasts.

Hatfield House, Great North Road, Hertfordshire AL9 5NQ.
Telephone: 01707 287010. Website: www.hatfield-house.co.uk
Tudor knot gardens created by Dowager Marchioness of Salisbury.

Holdenby House, Northampton NN6 8DJ.
Telephone: 01604 770074. Website: www.holdenby.com
Garden of plants from 1580 created by Rosemary Verey.

Kenilworth Castle and Elizabethan Garden, Castle Green, off Castle Road,
Kenilworth, Warwickshire CV8 1NE.
Telephone: 01926 852078.
Website: www.english-heritage.org.uk/daysout/properties/
kenilworth-castle
Stunning gardens created for Elizabeth I by her favourite, Robert
Dudley. Completely restored by English Heritage, including an aviary,
marble fountain and arbours.

Kentwell Hall, Sudbury, Long Melford, Sudbury, Suffolk CO10 9BA.
Telephone: 01787 310207.
Website: www.kentwell.co.uk
Tudor mansion with frequent re-enactments, including gardens
and gardeners. Collection of Tudor apple trees.

Lyveden New Bield, Lyveden, near Oundle, Northamptonshire PE8 5AT.
   Telephone: 01832 205358.
   Website: www.nationaltrust.org.uk/lyveden-new-bield
   Symbolic garden of Thomas Tresham, Catholic recusant. Moat, mounts,
   turf maze and orchards with banqueting house.
Melford Hall, Long Melford, Sudbury, Suffolk CO10 9AA.
   Telephone: 01787 376395.
   Website: www.nationaltrust.org.uk/melford-hall
   Banqueting house and terrace garden from the Tudor period.
Otley Hall, Hall Lane, Ipswich, Suffolk IP6 9PA.
   Telephone: 01473 890264. Website: www.otleyhall.co.uk
   Gardens recreated by Rosemary Verey, including mount, trellised
   garden and original moat.
Shakespeare Birthplace Trust
   Website: www.shakespeare.org.uk
   Series of houses and gardens associated with Shakespeare, some now
   planted with Tudor plants and designs.
Tudor House and Gardens, Bugle Street, Southampton, Hampshire SO14 2AD.
   Telephone: 023 8083 4242. Website: www.tudorhouseandgarden.com
   One of the first recreated knot gardens, now restored with heraldic
   figures on painted poles.

FURTHER READING

Beck, Thomasina. *Gardening with Silk and Gold*. David & Charles, 1997.
Campbell-Culver, Maggie. *The Origin of Plants*. Headline Publishing, 2001.
Gerard, John. *Herball* (facsimile edition). Bracken Books, 1985.
Harvey, John. *Medieval Gardens*. Batsford, 1981.
Henderson, Paula. *The Tudor House and Garden: Architecture and Landscape
   in the Sixteenth and Seventeenth Centuries*. The Paul Mellon Centre for
   Studies in British Art, 2005.
Jennings, Anne. *Tudor and Stuart Gardens*. English Heritage, 2005.
Martyn, Trea. *Elizabeth in the Garden*. Faber and Faber, 2008.
Rohde, Eleanour Sinclair. *The Story of the Garden*. The Medici Society, 1932.
Strong, Roy. *The Renaissance Garden in England*. Thames and Hudson,
   reprinted 1998.
Way, Twigs. *The Cottage Garden*. Shire Library, 2011.
Whalley, Robin, and Jennings, Anne. *Knot Gardens and Parterres*. Barn Elms
   Publishing, 1998.
Willes, Margaret. *The Making of the English Gardener*. Yale University
   Press, 2011.

INDEX